RR
RAVETTE PUBLISHING

This edition published by Ravette Publishing 2012.

ISBN: 978-1-84161-365-9

Save the Earth, it's the only planet with chocolate

Choccy Cheesecake

Ingredients

175g digestive biscuits

50g melted butter

300g quality cream cheese

200g mascarpone

200g melted white chocolate

200g melted milk chocolate

Method

1. Crush the biscuits and mix with the melted butter. Press the biscuit mixture into the base of a 20cm springform tin if making a large cheesecake or into ramekins if making single portions.

2. Carefully blend half the cream cheese with half of the mascarpone and do the same again so you have two separate mixtures

3. Fold the white chocolate into the cream cheese mix and spoon into the tin or ramekins and level off the top.

4. Fold the milk chocolate into the remaining cream cheese mix and spoon on top of the white chocolate already in place – you can even be daring and make nice patterns like we did!

5. Chill for 2 hours or overnight - if you can wait that long...

This cheesecake
is so easy
(and delicious too!)

Chocolate...
here today,
gone today

Chocalicious Cupcakes

Ingredients

150g softened butter

150g caster sugar

175g self-raising flour

50g cocoa powder

3 large eggs

1 tsp vanilla extract

Method

1. Heat the oven to 180°C/gas mark 4.

2. Line a 12 cupcake pan, with cupcake papers.

3. Gently break the eggs into a cup and beat lightly with a fork.

4. Place all the ingredients in a large bowl.

5. Beat with an electric mixer for 2 minutes, until light and fluffy.

6. Spoon the cupcake mixture evenly between the paper cases. This should make roughly 12 cupcakes depending on how big you like them!

7. Bake in the centre of the oven for 15 - 20 minutes until risen and firm to touch.

8. Leave to cool for a few minutes and then transfer to a wire rack.

9. Once completely cool you can decorate with frosting or icing and enjoy.

Men are like chocolates, wait too long and only the weird nutty ones are left

I never met a calorie I didn't like

You can cut the cake in half if you want filling but this truly decadent cake might only need a topping!

Wonderful White Chocolate Cake

Ingredients

250g butter

150g white chocolate

440g caster sugar

250ml milk

300g plain flour

1 tsp baking powder

1 tsp vanilla extract

2 eggs - lightly beaten

Topping/filling

125ml double cream

300g white chocolate, broken into small pieces

Method

1. Preheat oven to 180°C/gas mark 4. Lightly grease a DEEP 20cm round cake tin.

2. Put the chocolate, butter, sugar & milk in a saucepan and heat gently - stirring until smooth.

3. Leave the mixture to cool for a few minutes. With a whisk or a wooden spoon beat the flour into the chocolate mix, then add the eggs & vanilla extract.

4. Pour into the cake tin and cover with tin foil. Bake on middle shelf of the oven for 1 hour.

5. Remove the tin foil and leave the cake in the cake tin for 10 minutes before turning out onto wire rack to cool properly.

Topping/filling

1. Bring cream to the boil in pan then pour over the chocolate. Stir with a wooden spoon until the chocolate has melted. Leave to chill in the fridge for around 30 minutes - stirring occasionally then spread over the top and sides of the cake ... and YUM, you're done.

Exercise is a dirty word...
...everytime I hear it I wash
my mouth out with chocolate

Delicious Chocolate Brownies

Ingredients

100g butter

200g dark chocolate

4 medium eggs

250g golden caster sugar

100g plain flour

1 tsp baking powder

30g cocoa powder

Variations: Add any of the following to the final mix: 100g toasted roughly chopped hazelnuts or pecans; 2 handfuls of baby marshmallows; 100g small chocolate chunks; grated zest of an orange.

Method

1. Heat the oven to 180°C/gas mark 4. Line an 18-22cm square baking tin with greaseproof paper. Cut the butter into small pieces and break the chocolate up.

2. Melt both butter and chocolate together in a heatproof bowl set over a pan of simmering water. Cool to room temperature.

3. Whisk the eggs and sugar together until the mixture is light and fluffy.

4. Fold the chocolate mixture into the egg mixture and sift over the flour, baking powder and cocoa. Fold everything together with a metal spoon.

5. At this point you can add one or two of your favourite treats from the list above to make your brownies even more scrumptious.

6. Pour the mixture into the baking tray and bake for 25-30 minutes or until the top is cracked and the middle just set. Cool completely, then lift out of the tin and cut.

Why not drizzle melted chocolate over your cooked brownies... delish!

So much chocolate
so little time

Chocolate Chip Cookies

Ingredients

350g flour

1 tsp bicarbonate of soda

1 tsp salt

225g butter

175g caster sugar

175g soft brown sugar

1 tsp vanilla extract

2 eggs beaten

350g dark chocolate chips (or dark chocolate broken into small pieces)

Method

1. Preheat the oven to 190°C/gas mark 5.

2. Mix the flour, bicarbonate of soda and salt together in a small bowl.

3. In a larger bowl, beat the butter, both sugars and vanilla extract until creamy.

4. Beat in the egg mixture gradually.

5. Slowly stir in the flour mixture. Drop in the chocolate pieces and carefully combine.

6. Roll the mixture in your hands to create small golf ball sized shapes.

7. Place on baking tray and pat down gently making sure you leave plenty of space between each cookie.

8. Bake for 9-11 minutes.

9. Lift off tray with a spatula and cool slightly before serving.

Cookies

Chocolate is nature's way of making up for Mondays

Simple Chocolate Cake

Ingredients

175g caster sugar

175g softened butter

3 medium–large eggs

150g self-raising flour

1 tsp baking powder

50g of cocoa, sifted

1 tsp vanilla extract

pinch of salt

Frosting

100g (3½oz) of dark chocolate
100g (3½oz) of chopped butter

Method

1. Heat the oven to 180°C/gas mark 4. Lightly grease an 18cm (7in) round cake tin with small amount of butter. Draw around your cake tin and cut out a circle of greaseproof paper to line the tin with.

2. Put all of the ingredients in a large mixing bowl and beat with a mixer or a wooden spoon until smooth. (We said it was simple!)

3. Carefully pour the mixture into the tin, smoothing the top and place on the middle shelf in the oven. Leave for around 45-50 minutes. The cake should shrink slightly back from the edges of the tin and spring back if pressed lightly with your finger tip.

4. Leave in the tin to cool for a while before taking out of the tin to cool properly on a wire rack.

5. For the top of the cake, break the chocolate into small pieces and place along with the butter into a small heatproof bowl over a saucepan of simmering water until both have melted. Cool until it thickens slightly then spread over the cake top using a spatula.

I'd give up chocolate

but I'm no quitter

Trufflelicious!

Ingredients

280g good quality dark chocolate
(70% cocoa solids)

284ml pot double cream

50g unsalted butter

Flavouring

Grand Marnier, brandy, coconut liqueur or
the zest and juice of an orange.

Method

1. Break up the chocolate into small pieces and place in a bowl. Put the cream and butter into a saucepan and place on a gentle heat until the butter melts and the cream begins to simmer.

2. Remove from heat then pour over the chocolate. Stir the chocolate and cream together until you have a smooth mixture.

3. Add a favourite flavouring to the truffle mixture at this stage. Do this a teaspoon at a time until you like the taste. Cool and chill in a refrigerator for at least 4 hours.

4. To shape the truffles, dip a small spoon or melon baller in hot water and scoop up small balls of mixture, then roll between cocoa dusted palms and put the truffles onto greaseproof paper.

5. Coat your truffles immediately after you have finished shaping them. Use dessicated coconut, chopped nuts or chocolate vermicelli or leave them lightly dusted with cocoa powder. You could even dip them in melted chocolate.

Tip: Store in the fridge in an airtight container or freeze for up to a month. Defrost in the fridge overnight.

Truffles make great gifts! Place 6 or 8 truffles in a little box tied with pretty ribbon for a truly personal present.

Behind every successful woman

is a cat and a fridge full

of chocolate

Hot Chocolate Comfort

Ingredients

1 (70% cocoa solids) dark chocolate bar

1 pint of half-fat milk

1 small pot double cream

1 splash of brandy
(or your choice of alcohol - if desired)

Cinnamon or cocoa powder to sprinkle on top

Brown sugar (optional)

Method

1. Take the dark chocolate and break into small pieces. (Dark chocolate works better than milk chocolate as it has less fat content.)

2. Pour the milk into a saucepan and place over a gentle heat until it starts to steam. Make sure you don't boil the milk.

3. Add the chocolate and half of the carton of double cream. Simmer gently and stir continually until the desired consistency is reached. Pour into a food processor or use a hand whisk to froth it up.

4. At this point you can add extra sugar (to taste) and your alcohol option (if desired).

5. Top with whipped cream and a dusting of cinnamon or cocoa powder and enjoy...

If you want to
be particularly decadent,
how about topping it all off
with some whipped
cream !

Man cannot live by cake alone but woman can

Indulgent Chocolate Mousse

Ingredients

75g dark chocolate, broken into small pieces. Use a standard dark chocolate for this rather than chocolate with a high cocoa solid percentage as it will blend more thoroughly.

2 medium eggs, separated

25g butter, melted

2 tbsp caster sugar

1 tbsp Baileys or Tia Maria (this is optional)

To decorate

Ground nuts, cocoa, coconut, icing sugar, melted chocolate

Method

1. Melt the chocolate pieces in a bowl over a pan of boiling water.

2. Combine the melted chocolate with the egg yolks and butter.

3. Whisk the egg whites until nice and foamy and then whisk them into the sugar until the mixture is shiny and stiff.

4. Gently fold the two together with a metal spoon and also fold in the optional liqueur at this point.

5. Spoon into small serving glasses and garnish with a few dark chocolate curls or shapes.

The 3 step chocolate plan... never be more than 3 steps away from chocolate

White Chocolate Indulgent Fondue

Ingredients

200g good quality white chocolate, broken into small pieces

50g unsalted butter

142ml pot double cream

1 tsp vanilla extract or a splash of your favourite liqueur

250g of either chilled strawberries, raspberries, or marshmallows to dip and enjoy

Method

1. Combine the white chocolate, unsalted butter, double cream and vanilla extract in a heatproof bowl over a saucepan of simmering water.

2. Heat and stir until melted, shiny and smooth. Transfer to a fondue pot or warm saucepan and serve with chilled fruit or marshmallows.

friends are like fancy chocolates — it's what's inside that counts

Chocolate Cake Pops

Ingredients

1 packet basic cake mix

200g can buttercream frosting

300g chocolate (dark or milk)

To decorate

Edible glitter, chopped nuts or chocolate strands

Method

1. Follow cake mix recipe and when cake is cooked and cooled completely, crumble into large bowl and mix crumbled cake thoroughly with the can of buttercream frosting.

2. This can get a bit messy! Roll mixture into golf sized balls and place on the greaseproof paper (mixture should make about 12 pops).

3. Melt chocolate in a heatproof bowl over a simmering saucepan of water. When melted dip the tip of your lollipop stick in a little of the melted chocolate and gently push one halfway into each cake pop.

4. Place them in the freezer for a little while to firm up. Once firm, carefully insert the cake ball into the melted chocolate by holding the lollipop stick and very carefully swirling it around.

5. Once the pop is covered, remove and let excess chocolate drip back into the bowl.

6. Sprinkle with a little bit of your desired decoration. Enjoy mmmmmmmmmmmmm!

We've gone with a simple version. You could bake the cake entirely yourself first but the decoration takes a while so it's much easier to buy a packet of cake mix!

I am a woman
of many moods
and they all require
chocolate

Other BORN TO SHOP titles available ...

	ISBN	Price
All men are created equal... equally useless	978-1-84161-257-7	£4.99
Another day in paradise	978-1-84161-255-3	£4.99
Born to Shop Forced to Work	978-1-84161-348-2	£4.99
Born to Shop non Stop	978-1-84161-283-6	£4.99
Friends are the family we choose for ourselves	978-1-84161-254-6	£4.99
Gardening forever, housework whenever	978-1-84161-314-7	£4.99
I never met a calorie I didn't like	978-1-84161-256-0	£4.99
Life's too short to drink bad wine	978-1-84161-275-1	£4.99
M is for Mother, not for Maid	978-1-84161-274-4	£4.99
100% gorgeous ... most of the time	978-1-84161-284-3	£4.99

HOW TO ORDER   Please send a cheque/postal order in £ sterling, made payable to 'Ravette Publishing' for the cover price of the books and allow the following for post & packaging ...

UK & BFPO	70p for the first book & 40p per book thereafter
Europe & Eire	£1.30 for the first book & 70p per book thereafter
Rest of the World	£2.20 for the first book & £1.10 per book thereafter

RAVETTE PUBLISHING LTD
PO Box 876, Horsham, West Sussex RH12 9GH
Tel: 01403 711443   Fax: 01403 711554   Email: ravettepub@aol.com

Prices and availability are subject to change without prior notice.